Ultima Thule

Patterns Inspired by the Shetland Islands

Patterns by Denise Bell

Photographs and Essays by Chris Dykes

Lost City Knits

Hand-Dyed Yarns and Original Designs

www.lostcityknits.com

Table of Contents

Ultima Thule – a northernmost territory, a distant land, a remote ideal.

In May of 2014, Denise and I took a trip to the Shetland Islands of Scotland. I was a little apprehensive. What are we going to do there? What will we eat? Do they even have restaurants?

Yes, they have restaurants. They have an airport. A small airport, of course, so small and so snugly tucked into the southernmost tip of the island that the road to the terminal goes over a runway, and when a plane approaches someone goes out to put barriers across the road. Cars wait while planes take off and land.

Driving north on that road after the long flight of our first visit, we both fell in love with the place. We didn't know Shetland yet, but it immediately got to us. In the next days we saw exquisite lace on the northern-most Isle of Unst, saw ponies on the Isle of Yell, met with Oliver Henry at Jamieson & Smith Wool Brokers in Lerwick, and agreed to have our business, Lost City Knits, carry their Shetland Supreme yarns. We attended a meeting of the Shetland Spinners, Weavers, Knitters, and Dyers Guild. We took hikes. And we went out in sea kayaks with local guide Angus Nicol.

Denise, as she is wont to do, was working on designs the entire time. Travel has a way of opening up possibilities and creativity, and she was seeing ideas for lace designs throughout our trip.

Over the next year she sketched, charted, test knit, and completed the patterns in this book. In October of 2015 I returned to Shetland to photograph the garments in the environment that inspired them, and to slow down and spend more time with the people and the place.

This book is the product of our work. I've told the stories of some of the people I spoke with in my introduction, and each of Denise's patterns is prefaced both by her own inspirations and by short essays I wrote around the themes she was developing. The Shetland Museum provided old images of Shetland, each related to Denise's themes.

Of course we need to go back. We initially got to know the place, but now we know the people.

Chris Dykes

Stone. Soil. Water. Wool.

The place and the appeal are elemental. It's as though just enough was provided to make a go of it here. Homes could be built from stone; the ground, in the form of peat, could be burned for heat; crops could be grown for livestock, which would then provide food and wool for clothing. And, of course, there is the sea, which provided food and access to trade.

The people are elemental too, reflective of the land. There isn't much flash in how lifelong Shetlanders present themselves, and no one seems particularly interested in impressing anyone else.

Within the last several decades, however, a temptress has brought worldly trappings. The North Atlantic and North Sea are home to vast oil supplies, and oil is cited by Shetlanders as the biggest change the islands have experienced.

Shetlanders hate change. A waitress tells me that an alteration to a restaurant's menu can divide the population.

What has developed is a place with modern comfort and convenience but with traditions that continue to be part of the culture. As is the way of generational shifts, young people grow up with new technology and different ways of doing things. Being able to do by machine what used to be done by hand becomes a point of pride for the new generation, and the older generations wonder what is to become of the work that got them through their lives. Row boats get replaced by trawlers, produce from a croft (what Shetlanders call a small farm) gets replaced by inexpensive food at a supermarket, and intricately knitted colorwork can be programmed into a CAD machine and spit out in hours rather than months. What do the people think of the changes?

I've driven up a narrow driveway lined with rock walls. It's just wide enough for my tiny rental car. I soon learn that the space between those walls is plenty wide for Barbara Fraser's needs by design – she built them. Not owning a car, she gets around on a little scooter or on her four-wheeler. Barbara is a true, common-sense, hardworking, lifelong Shetlander. She was born on the Isle of Yell before there was a ferry to carry vehicles across, when a trip to Lerwick on the mainland and back home couldn't be completed without an overnight stay. Her family moved to the mainland when she was young because of this isolation. Today, ferries make the passage in thirty minutes carrying several automobiles.

When Barbara was growing up, the croft was an important part of the family's economy. Her father was a merchant seaman, so he had income from that work, but what the family grew and made themselves was essential. We are sitting in her kitchen having a cup of tea after she's showed me how she digs peat. A nearby stove burns peat dug in seasons past.

"It was important that we grew what we ate, rather than buying it. You grew up with the cycle of the seasons. Things had to be done. You had to get your potatoes in. If you wanted to eat potatoes in the winter, you had to get them planted. You had to keep them clean, weed-free," she says. Above the stove hang bags of kale seeds, drying to be sown next season.

"As wages improved, it was easier to go and buy stuff, and people lost interest in the croft. Unless you have a passion for growing things, it's difficult to get it back again. Someone buying a croft has to start from scratch, whereas if you grow up with it, you absorb it."

Barbara is known for the massive kale she's able to grow in her yard. She'll sell about six hundred kale seedlings to other crofters next spring, but she used to sell ten times that number. Instead of feeding kale to livestock, people now prefer to put out silage bales produced by machine. Young people aren't too interested in crofting, she says. There is too much money to be made at Sullom Voe, the center for the oil business in Shetland.

Tommy Isbister, another lifelong Shetlander, agrees. The first time I meet Tommy and Mary, his wife, they are preoccupied with sorting sheep. The second time I meet them is more condusive to conversation because we sit in the sunroom Tommy recently finished building off their living room on the Isle of Tronda. He began crofting on the land in the 1970s; then he and Mary moved there in 1977. Tommy has always worked with wood, first by building houses, followed by working on traditional Shetland wooden boats, and most recently by building violins and a cello. It's a curious fascination for a man who lives on an island largely without trees.

The best time on Shetland, he believes, was the 1960s. "Knittin' and fishin' were going strong. There was agriculture," he says, and Mary sighs. I'm not sure she's quite in agreement with her husband.

All of that changed in the 1970s with the discovery of oil in Shetland. "A lot of people thought oil would be a bad thing," Tommy says.

"You included," adds Mary.

"Money changed things. You used to be able to leave your keys in the car and no one would steal it," he says.

"You still can," Mary adds.

Tommy tells of a Shetlander who left his keys in his car, went about his business, and came back to an empty spot.

"That was forty years ago, Tommy," Mary reminds him.

"Yeah, but it didn't happen before," he says, unconvinced.

Oil did provide the public as a whole with money. The roads and bridges around Shetland are smooth and well-maintained. Towns have community centers and swimming pools. Still, worldly wants have changed the old ways.

"If that's what you want, makin' money at Sullom Voe, that's fine. But I would struggle to change what I have, not because I couldn't do it, but I just don't think that way," Mary says. "Everyone needs more now so crofters have a second job."

Mary leaves the room and comes back with a roll of parchment paper, which she carefully unrolls. From between the layers of paper emerges a fine lace shawl. There are some holes, but it is largely intact.

Tommy remembers his great-grandmother knitting it. He says the curators at the Shetland Museum looked at it, and they can't figure out how the edging was done. I ask if it were handspun, but Tommy doesn't remember. "She might have done," he says, and I think she probably did.

Knitting is one of the traditional crafts of Shetland, but the word craft seems too modern and too quaint a concept. Today, many use the word as a synonym for hobby. But knitting was work. Hard work. And it was an essential part of a family's economy.

Elizabeth Johnston operates Shetland Handspun out of Da Peerie Haa, or little house, attached to her home on the south mainland. She grew up knitting and spinning, but not as a hobby. It was always work. "Every woman my age on Shetland knits. I had to be different. All of my yarns are handspun." Whether customers buy skeins for their own work or fully finished Fair Isle cardigans, Elizabeth spins the fibers. Five spinning wheels and an electric spinner she uses for plying rest in her small living room, close to a small wood stove that puts out comfortable heat on a mild October day. Elizabeth uses the electric spinner for plying, not spinning. She wants the connection between foot and hand and fiber that only a traditional wheel can provide when she spins.

She stresses how important knitting was to her family when she was growing up. Knitters created items of value that could be sold or traded for other goods. If a knitter had better colors or a more interesting pattern, maybe her piece would be worth more. She points to a Fair Isle cardigan made of handspun yarn in her small shop. "That pattern is Fair Isle," she says, pointing to the crow's feet pattern, or OXO as it is sometimes known, "and that is traditional Shetland," pointing to peerie bands just above. "That is, before we pinched the other from Fair Isle."

According to Elizabeth, a merchant shipman liked the Fair Isle crow's feet pattern, but there weren't enough knitters on the small and remote Fair Isle to supply his needs, so he enlisted Shetland knitters to produce cardigans with that motif. Soon, everyone was knitting in the Fair Isle style. This would have been a hundred years ago, she says. Times change, a market opens, and people find a way to make money from their work.

Of her four children, only one is a knitter. Asked if that bothers her, if she's worried that her craft is in danger of becoming obsolete, she shakes her head. "No. Someone else will come along and do it." Indeed, when her granddaughter wanted a jumper made, Elizabeth gave her free reign on design. "She chose the color of the body and designed the yoke. She got it right even without being a knitter. You can't help but absorb this if you grow up around it."

Shetlanders need to know that they are marketable, that the place they come from is special and is of interest to others, Elizabeth says. She told a story of setting up a small booth at a craft fair, hanging elaborate lace pieces for customers to buy. Her young daughter was sort of helping and asked her mother if all of the pieces were for sale. Yes, Elizabeth said, and told her daughter to look at the price tag. The girl looked at the tag, gasped, looked again and gasped again, and said, "But…this has just been sitting around at the house!"

No longer does every Shetland woman knit. Clothing is cheap, replaceable, and the fashion industry sees to it that there is always a new style to buy. After Elizabeth tells me about Shetland College's Textile Department, I make a visit to their building on the north side of Lerwick. Roisin McAtamney, a first-year student in textiles, walks me around. She shows me a room full of hand framing machines from the 1990s. Students learn how to manipulate the machines to perform different knit stitches. I'm a bit taken aback, having spoken with Barbara and her kale seedlings, Tommy and Mary on their croft, and Elizabeth next to her spinning wheels. I'm accustomed to people who do their work by hand. Roisin then takes me to the next room, where two large machines, taking their direction from computers, churn out yards of colorwork to be made into mittens and hats.

This is the modern business of knitting on Shetland, I begin to understand. It is beautiful work and will make wonderful garments. And it's efficient. This is how one can make money producing finished garments in volume.

But it's not my association with Shetland. I understand, but I'm disillusioned.

Elizabeth Johnston told me that young women of Shetland need to stand up, show their talents, and understand that they, and the place they come from, have value in the marketplace.

On the day before I leave, I meet with Oliver Henry and Ella Gordon at Jamieson & Smith Wool Brokers in Lerwick. Oliver has been sorting and culling wool all of his life, and Jamieson & Smith buys eighty percent of the annual clip on Shetland. He's at an age where he'll soon be cutting back on work. A lot of wool has been sorted by Oliver in the past half-century.

Ella, on the other hand, is at the beginning of her career. In addition to working at the shop, Ella designs and markets her own patterns, often specifying Shetland wool as the preferred material. One of her signature motifs is of a roofless stone house, like those often seen from the roadways. Most people her age aren't in the fiber business, she says. There is too much money to be made working in oil or working in an office. But her passion about her home and her industry is strong. She believes in it, more than she believes in making a lot of money doing

something less interesting to her. Elizabeth was right not to fear a loss of interest in her craft. Someone else is coming along.

Not only is someone else coming along, but the older generation isn't done yet. Tommy doesn't work on big boats anymore, but he recently made a scale model of a traditional Shetland sixareen fishing boat that he races against a friend's model boat. Elizabeth laments that she is low on handspun Shetland wool and needs to get spinning to have a decent showing at her next festival.

And Barbara, having built the stone walls around her yard, has decided what to do with the leftover stone. Driving along Shetland's excellent roads, it's common to see stone pens set out by themselves or perhaps near the ruins of old, roofless houses. These are plantie crubs, used as enclosures that were safe from relentless wind and wandering sheep. A crofter would start kale seed inside a plantie crub in July of one summer, overwinter it, and then plant the young starts in a kale yard the following spring. Barbara has started building a new plantie crub, likely the only new one built on the islands in decades. She has dug the foundation, and the walls are now just over a foot tall. They'll be four feet by the time she's done.

"I'm hoping very much I'll be finished this winter. We'll see, we'll see. If not, then certainly by the next season."

Her soil and stone will wait.

Kishie Shawl

Asking a Shetlander about a kishie, the Shetland term for a large woven basket, is akin to asking someone about a record player. Yes, they are familiar with them. Every old house has one, but it's probably stashed away in an attic somewhere. Indeed, when asked, Barbara Fraser doesn't hesitate to rummage through her attic. Before I can change from my street shoes into the wellies she's provided for a mucky hike to dig peat, she returns with two beautiful baskets.

The smaller is a büddie which she made herself from docken grown in her yard. It's late in the season, but she finds a bit of docken in her yard and picks it, and then shows how to bend it into a useful shape for a container.

The kishie was given to her as a curio, and it is in very good condition. She doesn't use it the way Shetlanders did in the past, as a tool for carrying fish or peat.

She does, though, dig her own peat. October isn't the right season for digging, because the peat bricks won't have the summer to dry, but she offers to show how it's done. After a quarter mile hike uphill with one stop to catch some breath, we arrive at the spot she's been working on the past few years. "I don't tell anyone I'm going to dig peat because they always offer to help, and I don't want help," she says.

First, she uses a shovel to remove about six inches of topsoil, which she tosses down to ground that has already been harvested of peat. She places these pieces on previously exposed bedrock, so the peat can begin to rejuvenate. Then she gets behind the spot she's working on with a tusker, a wooden handled tool with a blade to cut peat on two sides. She pushes downward and then flips a piece of peat up to the level she's standing on. The motion comes easily after years of practice. She'll make a pile of the bricks and then turn the pile inside out in a few months. The peat will shrink dramatically as it dries.

Although kishies were once used to gather dried peat, Barbara uses her four-wheel ATV. The peat closet next to her garage is full, and she won't have to dig next year unless she just wants to stay ahead.

She burns peat in her stove all day, every day, year round. The stove probably dates to the 1950s, and when asked what purpose two pipes running into the back of it serve, she says that the stove also supplies her hot water. She used to have an electric water heater, but it was too much trouble to maintain.

Her büddie and kishie, once the preferred method of transporting peat, she'll keep around. That four-wheeler might give out some day.

(Opposite) Using a tusker to cut through peat and flip it up to ground level, where it will dry for several months before being brought to the peat closet (left). The natural fibers of a büddie (above).

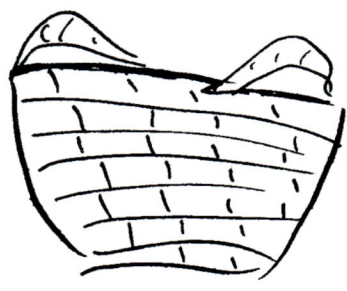

Kishie Shawl

The Kishie Shawl is a large triangle, featuring fish and net motifs.

A kishie is a traditional basket from Shetland -- one of many as I have learned in my research. They were made from straw and were quite durable. Many still exist today, although they are rarely used. When new, often having been made over the winter, a kishie would be used for market days, and as it got older would see duty carrying bait to a fishing outing, or a day's catch on the way back. As they became worn, kishies were often used to carry peat.

Fishing is certainly important to Shetland, but it was important in my house too, growing up. We lived near a lake, and my father saw to it that we always had crappie, sand bass, and striped bass in the freezer. Dad even ran a fishing guide service when I was in high school. He'd take customers out on the lake, and I'd come home from school to find them sitting around the kitchen table swapping stories. It was one of the first times I was aware of community being created from a common interest.

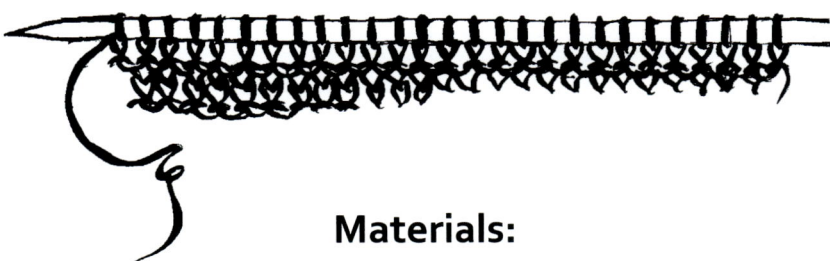

Materials:

Yarn: Lost City Knits Lost City Silk (1 skein)
Alternate Yarn: Jamieson & Smith Shetland Supreme 2 Ply Lace Weight (5 balls)
Yardage: 1000 yards / 914 meter
Color Shown in Sample: Pretty Penny and Artemesia
Needle Size: 4 US / 3.5 mm circular or straight needle
Small cable needle or sock needle
Finished Size 80 inches / 203 cm wingspan

BASIC INSTRUCTIONS

Kishie is a top-down triangle shawl, and has two outer edge stitches on each side that are **not included in the charts**. Edging stitches are always knit, never purled. (Many knitters like to slip the first stitch of every row as if to purl for a clean edge. The choice is yours.) The charts also do not include the center stitch. This triangle shawl increases by 4 stitches every odd-numbered (RS) row. In some cases, these increases are created by yarn overs, and in some cases they are created by knitting into the front and back of a stitch (kfb). **These increases are charted**.

This shawl starts with 5 stitches building on a stockinette base to 33 stitches total where we begin the Basket Weave chart. Next is the Cod and Current chart, which is repeated 6 times. The Drops chart is knit as an applied edging. **Each chart has a few extra notes of instruction, so please be sure to read these notes before beginning the chart.**

Cast On and Set Up

Cast on 5 stitches using your preferred method, leaving a 6-inch tail which will be woven in after blocking.

SET UP
Row 1 - k, yo, kfb, k, kfb, yo, k. (9 stitches)
Row 2 - k2, p5, k2.
Row 3 - k2, yo, k1, kfb, k, kfb, k1, yo, k2. (13 stitches)
Row 4 - k2, p9, k2.
Row 5 - k2, yo, k3, kfb, k, kfb, k3, yo, k2. (17 stitches)
Row 6 - k2, p13, k2.
Row 7 - k2, yo, k5, kfb, k, kfb, k5, yo, k2. (21 stitches)
Row 8 - k2, p17, k2.
Row 9 - k2, yo, k7, kfb, k, kfb, k7, yo, k2. (25 stitches)
Row 10 - k2, p21, k2.
Row 11 - k2, yo, k9, kfb, k, kfb, k9, yo, k2. (29 stitches)
Row 12 - k2, p25, k2.
Row 13 - k2, yo, k11, kfb, k, kfb, k11, yo, k2. (33 stitches)
Row 14 - k2, p29, k2.

Begin Basket Weave Chart

In Basket Weave, both sides of the fabric are charted. You will see that the even-numbered (WS) rows are not pure rest rows and require a bit of your attention. I found that using a small wooden double-point sock needle worked well as a cable holder. The increases for this chart consist of yarn overs and kfbs, both of which are charted.

When working this chart, you will work the first section of the shawl reading from right to left on the odd (RS) rows and left to right on the even (WS) rows. Knit the **uncharted** center stitch. Then work this chart as a mirror image, left to right for the odd (RS) rows and right to left for the even (WS) rows. (Yes, that means the cables too, which is called reverse twining according to my contemporary basket-making buddies.) Work Rows 1-24 of the Basket Weave chart, then repeat Rows 17-24 (repeating the stitches within the red box) until 94 stitches are in each section (excluding the edging stitches and center spine). 193 stitches total.

Basket Weave Chart

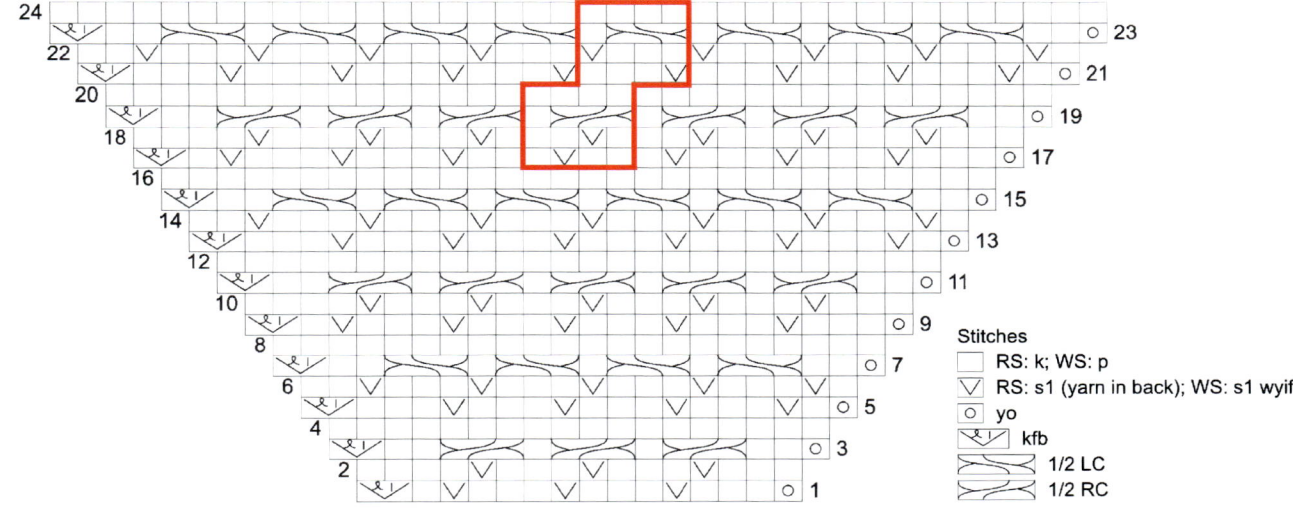

Stitches

☐	RS: k; WS: p
∨	RS: s1 (yarn in back); WS: s1 wyif
○	yo
kfb symbol	kfb
	1/2 LC
	1/2 RC

Begin Cod and Current Charts

These original charts depict fish in open water, with the current flowing around them. They make up the main body of the shawl. Cod and Current has **uncharted** rest rows on the WS of the fabric which are purled. Once again, I found that using a small wooden double-point sock needle worked well as a cable holder.

The increases are yarn overs for this part of the shawl instead of kfb, and are included in the two charts. Why two charts? In this particular instance, I found that creating a mirror image chart was more helpful than the method of trying to reverse the chart as I work, which was easily done in the Basket Weave chart. So - knit the edging stitches, work the RIGHT SIDE section, knit the center stitch, work the LEFT SIDE section, knit the edging stitches. Note - there are a few rows where the chart increases more than just the edging stitches! Also note - if you are using markers to designate pattern repeats, there are a few rows when you will need to slip a marker to adjust the repeat. It's a wee bit fiddly but it's not difficult. The stitch legend is the same for both charts. The stitches within the red box are the pattern repeat.

Work Rows 1-18 of the Cod and Current chart 6 times. (457 stitches total)

SET UP after completing the Cod and Current charts –
Next row (RS) knit 1 row decreasing 6 stitches evenly. (451 stitches total)
Next row (WS) k2, purl until 2 stitches remain, k2.

Stitches

☐	k
○	yo
╱	k2tog
╲	ssk
⋌	s1-k2tog-psso
	3/2 RC
	3/2 LC

RIGHT SIDE SECTION

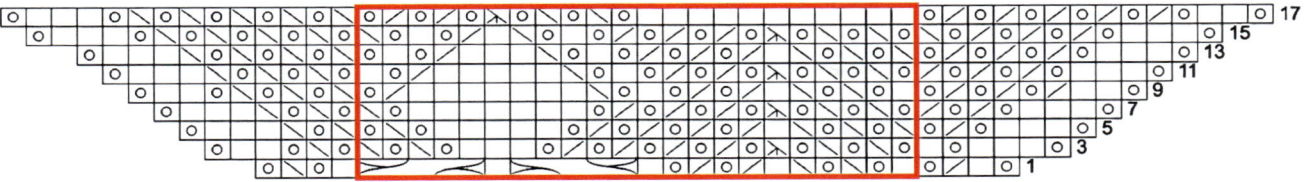

LEFT SIDE SECTION

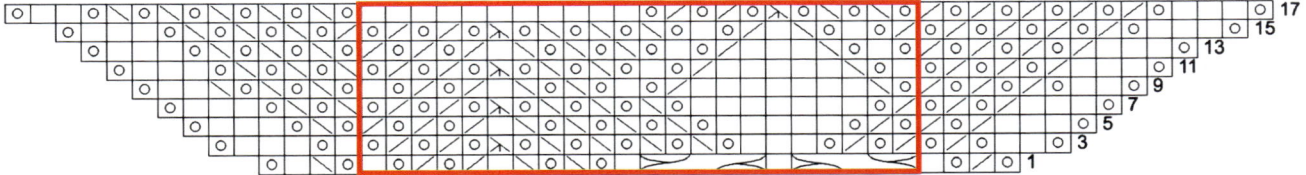

Begin Drops Chart

This wonderful traditional Shetland pattern is an applied edging at the lower edge of the shawl. Even-numbered (WS) rows contain a minor amount of patterning. Note that Rows 1-7 and Row 20 increase on the outermost edge on both the RS and the WS by knitting into the front and back of the stitch. The yarn overs are done back to back by wrapping the yarn over the needle twice. On the subsequent row, knit into the first yarn over, purl into the second.

Without binding off the last WS row of the previous chart, and with the RS facing you, cast on 19 additional stitches using a knitted cast on. Work Row 1, which begins at the far edge of the previously cast on stitches, working back to the body of the shawl, slipping the last stitch. Turn your work. For Row 2 begin by purling the next stitch from the body of the shawl together with the first stitch of the edging. This method joins the body of the shawl to the edging and will be done on each WS row, slowly finishing off the stitches of the shawl. In effect you are binding off by adding the edging. Work rows 1-20 of the Drops chart 45 times, until 1 stitch from the body of the shawl remains. Knit back towards the body of the shawl, loosely binding off each stitch as you go. When only 1 stitch of the edging remains, knit it together with the final shawl body stitch. Cut your working yarn and pull the stitch through. Weave in this tail after blocking.

Note that this chart is knit using a garter stitch base, not a stockinette stitch base. Therefore, all blank cells in the chart are knit. A purl is represented by a bold dot in the cell.

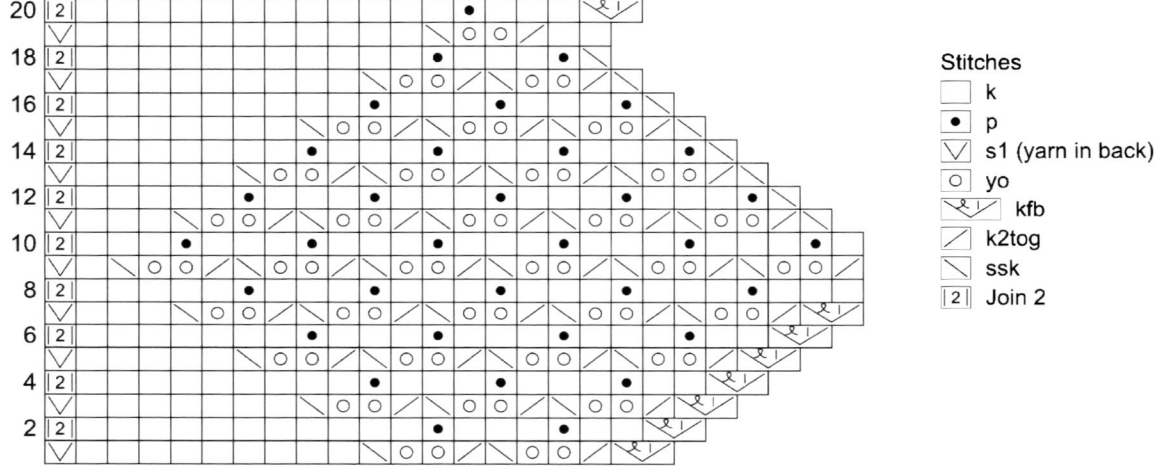

Stitches

□	k
•	p
∨	s1 (yarn in back)
○	yo
⅂	kfb
∕	k2tog
＼	ssk
‖2‖	Join 2

15

Lerwick Harbour Hap

The warehouse is full of fish.

Three boats have unloaded four days worth of catch, and boxes of cod, haddock, catfish, monkfish, and others sit in the warehouse on ice, waiting for the daily fish auction to begin. Each boat has an onboard icemaker, and as fish are caught, they are put in crates and iced to be unloaded later at this warehouse on a dock at the Lerwick Harbour.

It should be a record year, according to Ewen MacRitchie, a manager at Lerwick's Shetland Seafood Auction fish market. At 8:00 in the morning the daily fish auction begins. Wholesalers speak with clients in mainland Europe, determining how much they want to spend on the different lots of fish. The auction accepts online bids as well. These clients, in turn, will sell the fish to restaurants.

The auction runs backwards. Instead of bidding starting low and ending with the two highest bidders waiting each other out, the bidders enter what they are willing to pay until the price drops to the highest bid. This is for business, not for show, and the drama of a traditional auction would just slow down the action.

A ton of fish can sell for around £800. One of these ships can contain a thousand tons of fish. It's big business. The second biggest ship docked in the Lerwick Harbour in October is the ADENIA. It was recently overhauled and had a center portion added to increase its holding capacity. More space means more fish and more money. About four or five men will go out on an eighty-foot boat, but Ewen says they usually aren't Shetlanders anymore. Most of them are from the Philippines or Eastern Europe.

The Shetlanders, he says, now work in the oil industry. Money is better and workers get to go home at night. And while the ADENIA is the second largest ship docked at the harbor, the largest is the SANS VITESSE, a cruise ship converted to house workers for the oil industry. No one much talks about the cruise ship, as if it's seen as a necessary compromise for the income that oil provides. Several people mention the ADENIA, though, and the risk its owners took in increasing its capacity.

As I heard Shetlanders say often of traditional work, if you grow up with it, you absorb it.

Not every Shetland shawl is made from fine yarn and can pass through a wedding ring. Shetland's weather can be rough, and the practical Shetlanders know that thick wool offers protection from wind and rain. The traditional hap shawl is called for when one's needs turn from lace to warmth.

The first evening we were in Shetland we walked down to the harbour and got a bite to eat at the chippy shop. We sat outside on metal chairs, and I watched and listened to the boats tied up in the harbour. I saw colorful ropes anchoring ships to the dock.

Whereas a traditional hap would be made from natural greys, browns, and whites, for my full-sized hap I decided on a splash of color. Note the non-typical cable on the applied edging of the full sized hap that alters it from the usual garter-stitch two-sided hap to a one-sided shawl. The half hap pattern, which follows the full hap, has a non-cabled edging and is reversible.

Materials:

Full Hap (square)
Yarn: Lost City Knits Foothills Fingering Merino (1750 yds / 1600 meters total)
Yardage: MC 1120 yds, CC1 115 yds, CC2 300 yds, CC3 20 yds, CC4 115 yds
Colors Shown in Sample: MC Vintage 387, CC1 Spring Valley VFD, CC2 Burnt Earth, CC3 Hispaniola, CC4 River Mud
Needle Size: 6 US / 4mm 32 and 47 inch length circular needle
Finished Size: Approximately 40 inches / 101 cm per side, 65 inch / 165 cm wingspan
Half Hap (triangle)
Yarn: Jamieson & Smith Shetland Supreme Jumper Weight (750 yds / 686 meters total)
Yardage: MC 630 yds, CC1 150 yds, CC2 70 yds
Colors Shown in Sample: MC 2009 Yuglet , CC1 2005 Shetland Black, CC2 2001 White
Needle Size: 6 US / 4mm 32 and 47 inch length circular needle
Finished Size: Approximately 64 inch / 162 cm wingspan

BASIC INSTRUCTIONS

Traditional Shetland Hap Shawls are square and are worked from the center out. Modern knitters enjoy a variety of options, so with this in mind I've included both a square shawl and a top-down triangle shawl. Both are worked in garter stitch, creating a thick, warm garment to ward off a chilling wind. Whether you decide to make a shawl using bright colors or natural sheep colors is up to you.

LERWICK HARBOUR - FULL HAP VERSION

Begin Center Diamond

Using Main Color (MC), knit a diamond shape as follows: Begin with 1 stitch, leaving a 6-inch tail, increase 1 stitch EVERY row (both RS and WS) in the following method until you have 112 stitches. Then decrease 1 stitch EVERY row in the following method until you once again have 1 stitch.

- Increasing method: *Yarn over, knit to the last stitch, knit into the back of the loop of the last stitch*. Turn and repeat until you have 112 stitches.
- Decreasing method: *Yarn over, s1k2togpsso, knit to the last stitch, knit into the back loop of the last stitch*. Turn and repeat until 2 stitches remain. K2tog, leaving 1 stitch on the needle.

For the first side, pick up and knit 55 stitches after the remaining live stitch. Pick up and knit 56 stitches on each of the remaining sides. While the previous portion was knit flat, you will now begin knitting in the round. To help keep you on track, stitch markers should be placed at each corner to section off the 4 sides of the shawl, which are also the 4 repeats of the Old Shell chart.

Purl 1 round even.
Knit 1 round increasing in the following manner for each of the 4 sections: yo, knit until 1 stitch remains, yo, k1. Work the previous 2 rounds above 2 more times, until you have 62 stitches per section.

Set Up
Row 1 – work *yo, k2tog* around.
Row 2 – purl 1 round even.

Begin Old Shell Chart

You will be changing colors several times throughout this portion of the shawl, which means you will have ends to weave in. What? You don't like weaving in ends, or the jog that occurs when colors are changed? A simple solution is to use the time-honored spit splice as a join. (Wet felting is a more delicate term, if you prefer not to refer to saliva.) My method for this maneuver is to knit to the end of the last round of a color and cut my yarn, leaving only an inch and holding it carefully so it doesn't slip out. Then I tink (unknit) back about 10 stitches and spit splice, joining the new color before reknitting those stitches. Usually the joined colors occur over several stitches and are only noticeable for one round. By the time I work the second and third rounds, the colors meld nicely. Listed below are the color-sequence changes used in the original pattern shown in the photos.

MC Rounds 1-3
CC1 Rounds 4-10
CC2 Rounds 11-27
CC3 Rounds 28-34
CC4 Rounds 35-40

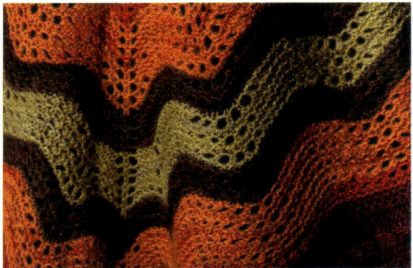

This shawl pattern is garter-stitch based, however you can knit it stockinette based if you so desire.
What does that mean? That means, for the charts that follow, even-numbered rest rounds are knit, not purled, unless otherwise noted in the stitch legend that follows each chart.

Old Shell - Traditional Interior Border Chart

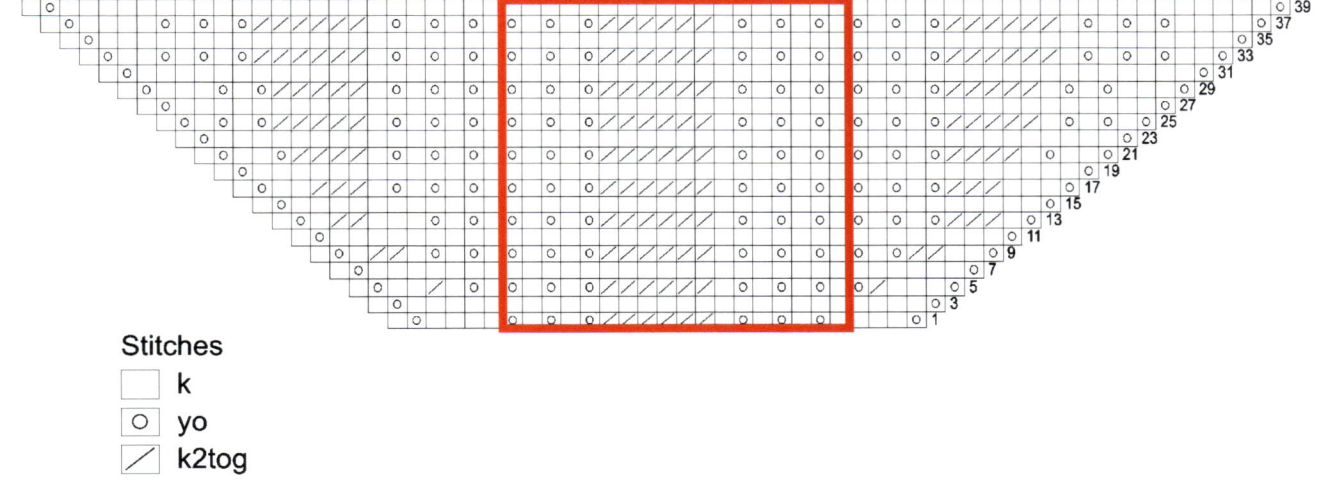

Stitches

☐	k
☐ (o)	yo
☐ (/)	k2tog

Work rounds 1-40 of the Old Shell chart, repeating the stitches within the red box 3 times - 4 times around. Then begin the chart again on Round 5, repeating the stitches in the red box 5 times. This time you will be reversing the color sequence as listed below.

CC4 Rounds 5-10
CC3 Rounds 11-18
CC2 Rounds 19-34
CC1 Rounds 35-40

Repeat Rounds 39-40 once more, using MC
(140 stitches per section, 560 stitches total)
Knit 1 round even with MC.
Cut your yarn, leaving a 24-inch tail.

Begin Rope and Wave Chart - Applied Edging

Begin the Rope and Wave chart by casting on 23 stitches using MC. A provisional cast on will allow a nice graft at the completion of the edging. Be sure to leave a long tail. I suggest 24-28 inches. The applied edging can be knit as garter or stockinette, as with the previous chart.

*(The very first time you knit Row 1, **knit** the first and last stitch in that row. If you were to slip it, as per the symbol, you would be slipping the provisional yarn! You don't want that.)*

The next chart joins one stitch from the body of the shawl to the edging on every even-numbered or wrong-side (WS) row by purling it together with a slipped stitch from the edging stitches. This is the Join 2 noted in the chart. Each time you purl a slipped stitch together with a stitch from the body, you are in effect binding off a stitch of the shawl.

Rope and Wave Chart

Key:
- ☐ RS: k; WS: p
- • RS: p; WS: k
- ⋁ s1
- ○ yo
- ╱ k2tog
- ╲ ssk
- ⟋⟍ 2/2 RC
- |2| WS: Join 2

Work Rows 1-16 of the Rope and Wave chart until 1 stitch from the body of the shawl remains, ending on Row 15. Purl the Join 2 as usual, then move that stitch back to the left needle. After this you should have 23 stitches on your needle. Cut your yarn, leaving a 24-inch tail to secure later. Remove the provisional cast on and return the 23 live stitches to a second needle. We'll use several versions of the Kitchener stitch to bind off. Why? Because the edging has garter stitch, stockinette stitch, and purled areas. It didn't seem that complicated while you were knitting, did it? It wasn't, but we want a nice bind off that doesn't detract from the established pattern. It's easy, don't worry!

For the stitches in garter (those that lead up to the purls before the cable), you will need to graft in garter. Holding the wrong sides facing one another, graft BOTH the front and back needle as follows: knit off, purl on.

For the purled stitches flanking the cable, graft as follows: For the front needle, purl off, knit on. For the back needle, knit off, purl on.

For the 4 cable stitches, use the standard Kitchener stitch as follows: For the front needle, knit off, purl on. For the back needle, purl off, knit on.

Now secure the working yarn with a few whips through stitches on the body of the shawl and trim leaving a 6-inch tail.

Here's a link to a very good tutorial on grafting in pattern. *(Used with permission.)*

https://lucyintheskywithstitches.wordpress.com/2013/02/26/tutorial-grafting-in-pattern/

Gently wet block your shawl, pinning out the points. After it is thoroughly dry, weave in all of the loose ends.

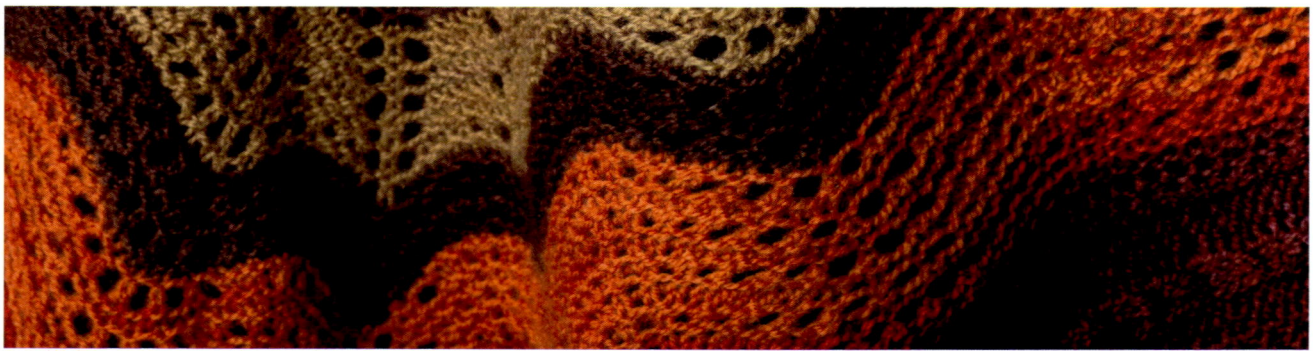

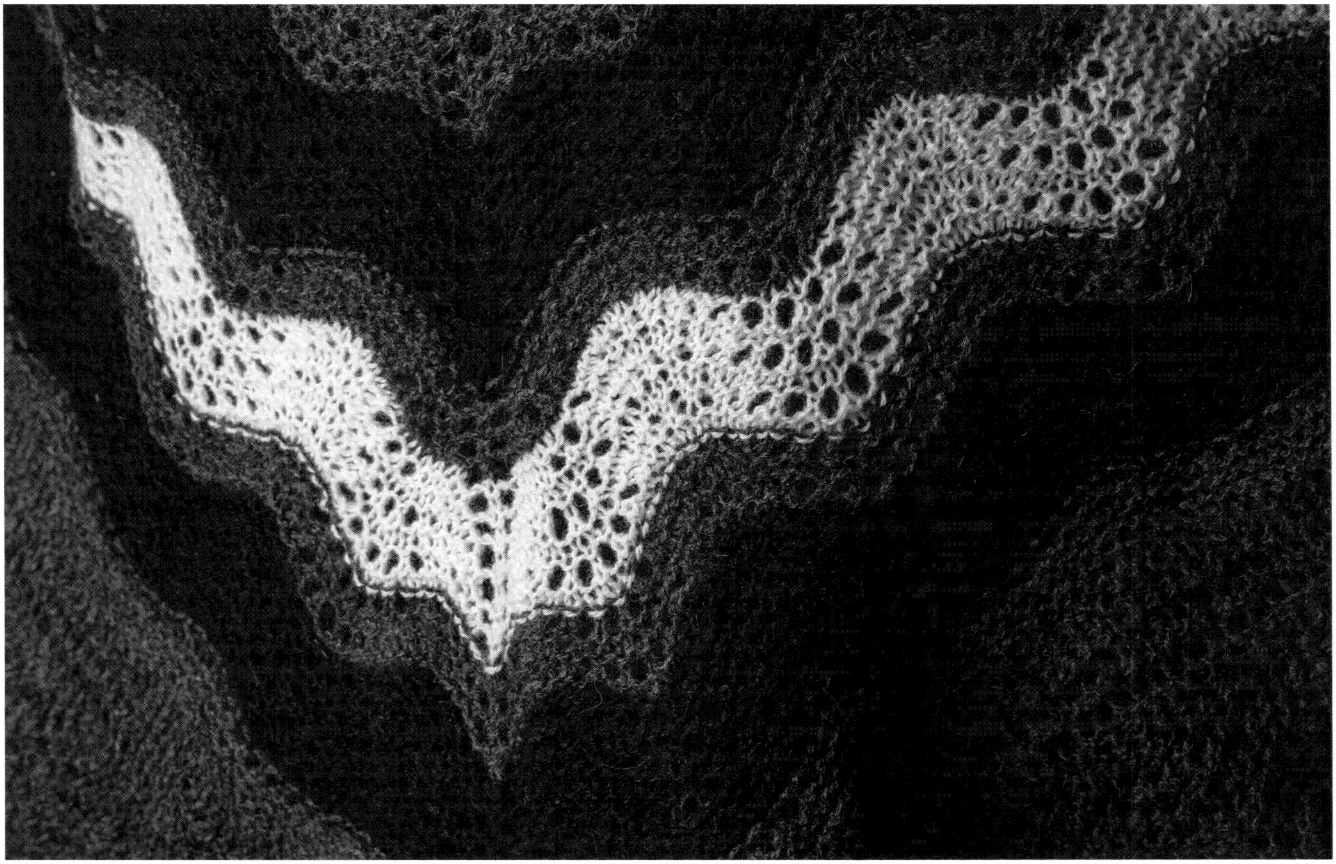

LERWICK HARBOUR – HALF HAP VERSION

Begin Center Triangle

Using Main Color (MC), knit a triangle shape: Begin with 1 stitch, leaving a 6-inch tail. Increase 1 stitch EVERY row, both RS and WS, in the following method until you have 116 stitches.

- Increasing method: *Yarn over, knit to the last stitch, knit into the back loop of the last stitch*. Turn and repeat until you have 116 stitches. Do not cut or break working yarn.

Finish the top edge of your shawl in a way that will visibly flow into the next chart in a pleasing manner, as follows: k, work *yo, k2tog* until 1 stitch remains, yo, k (single stitch increased.) Knit 1 row even. Bind off loosely until 1 stitch remains. With RS facing pick up and knit into each yarn over along the lower 2 sides of the triangle (RS). Knit 1 row increasing to 123 stitches. Knit 1 row even.

Mark RS with a contrasting, removable marker to help you keep track of RS and WS.
Next row (WS) - k2, place marker (pm), k61, pm, k1, pm, k61, pm, k2. (127 stitches)

You have now delineated 2 flanking edge stitches on each side of the triangle, and a center stitch. The flanking edging stitches DO NOT appear on the chart below. The center stitch is designated in BLUE. Standard knitting is to knit the edging stitches, then work the chart beginning at Row 1 (read right to left), including the blue center stitch, work the chart again (without the center stitch), then knit the edging stitches. Only RS rows are charted. All WS rows are knit. We are creating a shawl based on a garter-stitch background. If you prefer, reverse the decrease stitches (work ssk instead of k2tog) on the second half of the shawl.

Begin Old Shell Chart

To match the black, white, and gray shawl shown in the photo, change colors in the sequence below.

Rows 1-10 gray
Rows 11-27 black
Rows 28-34 gray
Rows 35-40 white

Work Rows 1-40 of the Old Shell chart, repeating the stitches within the red box 3 times. Then begin the chart again on Row 5, repeating the stitches within the red box 5 times. This time you will be reversing the color sequence as listed below, creating a mirror image of the color changes.

Rows 5-11 white
Rows 12-18 gray
Rows 19-35 black
Rows 36-40 gray
Repeat Rows 39-40 once more (281 stitches total)

Old Shell Chart

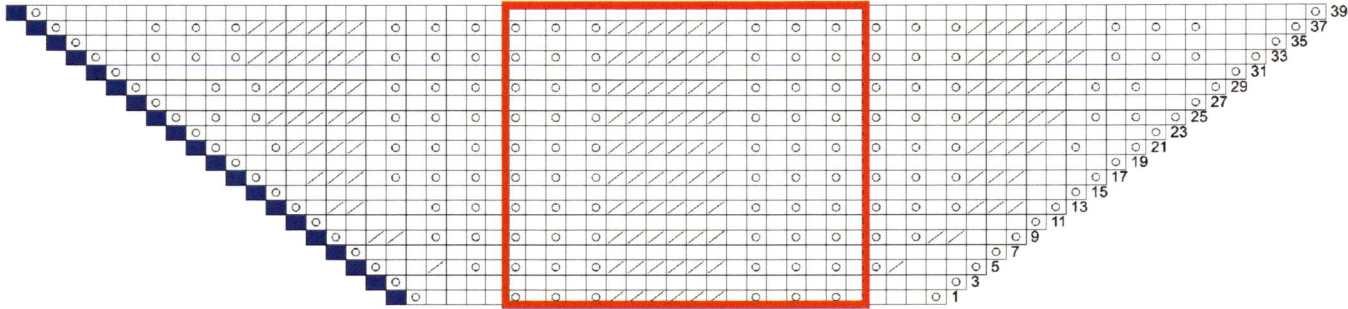

Yarn

	Repeat Chart On Each Side Of Center Stitch
(blue)	Center Stitch

Stitches

	k
o	yo
/	k2tog

Some people enjoy the wavy look of Old Shell and prefer to keep it as the lower edge of the shawl. Some people prefer an applied edging. Both are acceptable in traditional Shetland haps. If you want to add an applied edging, a nice and easy one is supplied below.

Scalloped Lace Chart - Applied Edging

After completing the Old Shell chart, do not cut the yarn. Begin the Scalloped Lace chart by casting on 19 stitches with your working yarn. I use a knitted cast on, also called a cable cast on, for this purpose. The applied edging is knit in garter stitch.

The next chart joins one stitch from the body of the shawl to the edging on every even-numbered or WS row by purling it together with a slipped stitch from the edging stitches. This is the Join 2 noted in the chart. Some people see this as a sideways added edging, which is an apt description of how it is applied to the body of the shawl. Each time you purl the slipped stitch together with a stitch from the body you are in effect binding off a stitch of the shawl.

Work rows 1-16 of the Scalloped Lace chart. You will work a total of 35 repeats until 1 stitch from body of the shawl remains and 19 stitches of the edging remain. Loosely bind off those stitches in the standard manner, working towards the body of the shawl. Knit the last stitch together with the last body stitch of the shawl. Cut your yarn, leaving a 6-inch tail. Weave in this tail after blocking.

Scalloped Lace Chart

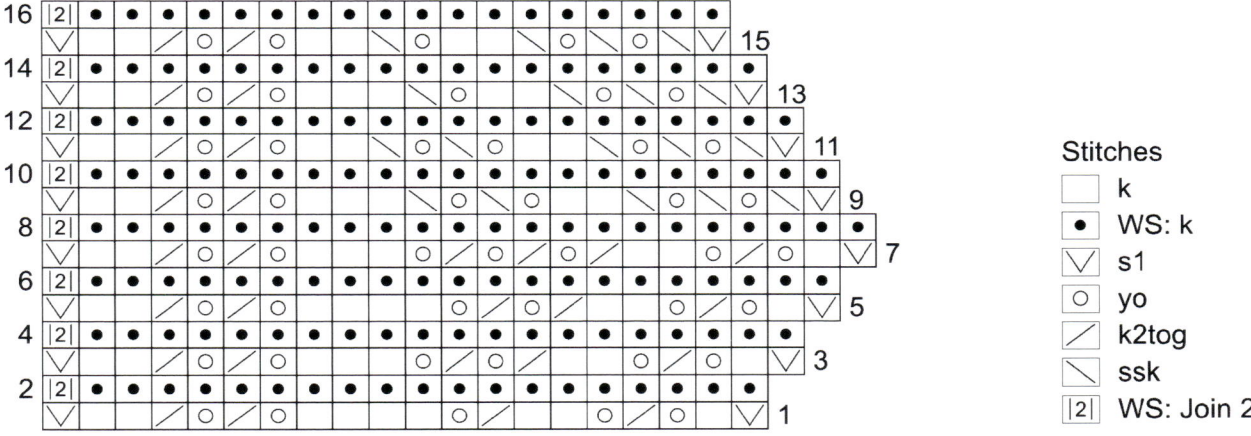

Stitches

☐	k
●	WS: k
∨	s1
○	yo
╱	k2tog
╲	ssk
|2|	WS: Join 2

Voe Cowl

From the sunroom he recently added onto the house he built forty years ago, Tommy Isbister and his wife Mary look out over the waters of the North Atlantic. Tommy has always been building something or other. He began his career as a joiner, building wooden house frames, but he wanted to work on boats. There was only one floundering boat builder on the island when he was about to go to work, and he was advised not to join that shop. So he built houses instead.

He learned of a fellow who would build and work on boats at night, and Tommy started to hang around him, watching and learning. Before long he was building more boats than houses.

The traditional Shetland fishing boat is the wooden sixareen, or sixern, as the word is pronounced, so named because it was a six-oared boat, with three men on each side rowing anywhere from ten to forty miles offshore. It's common to see these boats, or a smaller version called a foureen, in yards that border a voe, as Shetlanders call an inlet or bay. The last sixareen built for the Shetland fishing industry was made in the 1880s. The weather and waters of Shetland require bigger and safer vessels. As technology improved, the old boats became obsolete.

Tommy has built or restored countless traditional boats. Shetland is home to many elemental things, but plentiful wood is not one of them. Many of the traditional Shetland boats were assembled in Norway, built from Norse Larch trees, and then shipped to Shetland for reassembly, somewhat like an IKEA bookcase.

Tommy's great-grandfather built the boat that is currently housed in the Shetland Museum in Lerwick. The boat was used to deliver mail to the even more remote Isle of Foula.

Today, Tommy's boat-building days are probably over. Instead, he has turned his attention and talents to constructing violins and cellos. He tells the story of a neighbor calling to ask if he'd like some wood from a maple tree that was being cut down. Tommy took a bit of the trunk, and in time made a violin from the wood.

A Shetlander who had moved to Minnesota in the United States was visiting and reminiscing with Tommy about the property he used to own there

and the trees he had planted. Tommy knew of the man's land and knew who had bought it. Tommy asked if he had by chance planted a maple tree years ago. He had. Tommy retrieved the violin and told his friend that it had been made from the tree he had planted. His friend bought the violin for his granddaughter.

On good days Tommy thinks he might build another boat, but on other days he thinks he's done. The violins and cellos are enough, and playing music with Mary overlooking the voe is a good way to spend an evening.

The past isn't far behind on Shetland, though, and every morning a boat he built in 1992 passes by on the waters just outside his house.

Tommy next to the last boat he built, and in his shop demonstrating a tool Norwegians use to route lumber and place nails in the correct position.

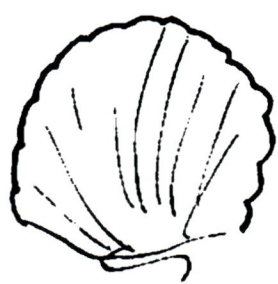

Voe Cowl

The word voe in Shetland refers to a small inlet. In these areas where the seawater rushes against the land, abandoned cockleshells can be plentiful on the beaches, and in the fields and pastures, left there by larger storms.

We took a hike along the shore the day before we left Shetland. We passed through gates and climbed over stiles to cross fences, all of which were part of a series of public paths referred to as Shetland Access Routes. These paths often cross private land, and are created and maintained for the public good. I picked up several cockleshells as token reminders of our hike, and they now sit on a bookshelf at home.

The natural and the human worlds meld on Shetland, and Voe is also the name of a community on the mainland. During our visit we were fortunate enough to be invited to the monthly meeting of the Shetland Spinners, Knitters, Weavers, & Dyers Guild. In the little community center in Voe we met with about twenty Shetland knitters. Their lace, colorwork, and kindness still inspire.

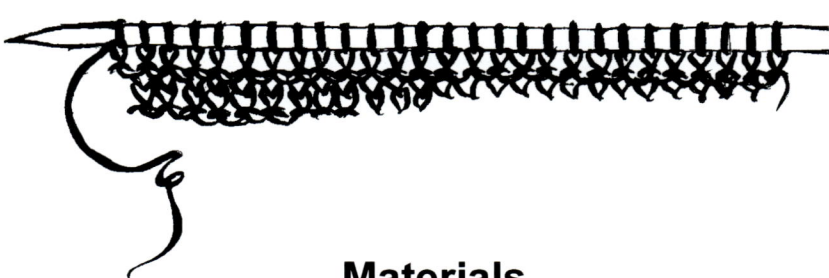

Materials

Yarn: Jamieson & Smith Shetland Supreme 1 Ply Lace Weight Cobweb (1 ball)
Alternate Yarn: Lost City Knits North Pasture Alpaca (1 skein)
Yardage: 320 yards / 292 meters (J&S) 350 yards / 320 meters (LCK)
Colors Shown in Samples: White (J&S), Grey (J&S), and Desert Rose (LCK)
Needle Size: US 2 / 2.75 mm circular 24 inch
Finished Size: 24 inches / 61 cm circumference

BASIC INSTRUCTIONS

Two charts are included in this pattern. The first is a modified version of the cockleshell motif that I devised, depicting the ridges of the shell. The second is the traditional Shetland cockleshell stitch.

Begin Cockleshell Chart

Cast on 168 stitches using your preferred method for 8 repeats of the entire chart or, if a wider cowl is desired, increase by 21 stitches for each additional cockleshell. Each shell is approximately 3 inches wide when blocked. Leave a 6-inch tail to be woven in after blocking. Join for knitting in the round.

Knit 1 round.
Purl 1 round.

IMPORTANT INSTRUCTION NOTE:

When slipping the purled stitches on Round 11, drop the double yarn overs between the 14 purled stitches, being sure to slip the purled stitch after the last double yarn over for a total of 15 slipped stitches. Transfer the 15 stitches back to the left needle, **THEN** purl the cluster together as one stitch before executing the rest of the stitches on that round. It is a tricky maneuver; take the time to make sure every one of the slipped stitches is caught when purling them together. A dropped stitch will ladder back and ruin the exacting work you've accomplished.

Modified Cockleshell

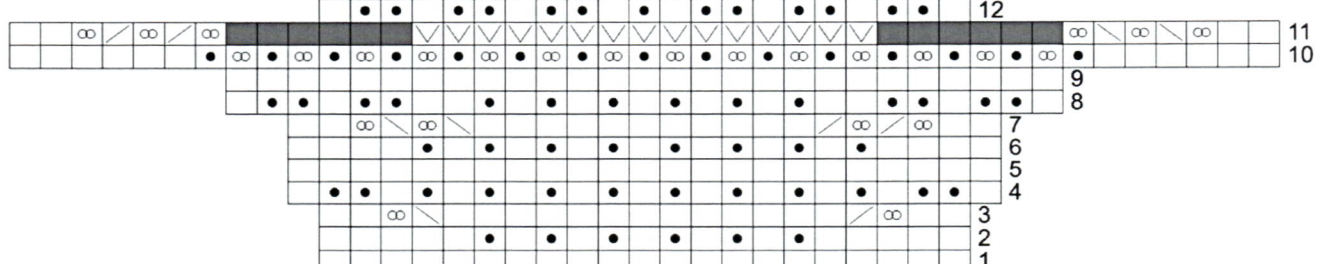

Modified Cockleshell

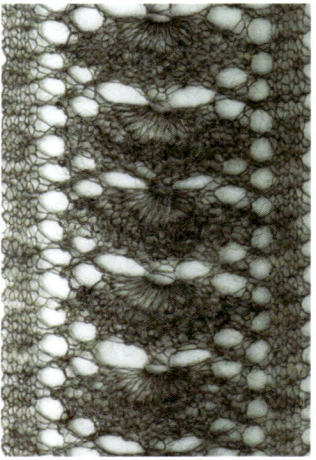

Traditional Cockleshell

33

Traditional Cockleshell

Stitches

⬛	No stitch
☐	k
•	p
⋁	s1
⁄	k2tog
⟍	k2tog-b
∞	Double Yarn Over

Work 12 repeats of the 12 rounds of the desired chart. After completing your last horizontal repeat of the chart, knit 1 round, purl 1 round, then bind off loosely. Gently wet block your cowl. For blocking the sample cowls, I used a posterboard taped together as a tube and covered with plastic cling wrap. The scalloped curves of the cockleshell edging were pinned open using T-pins.

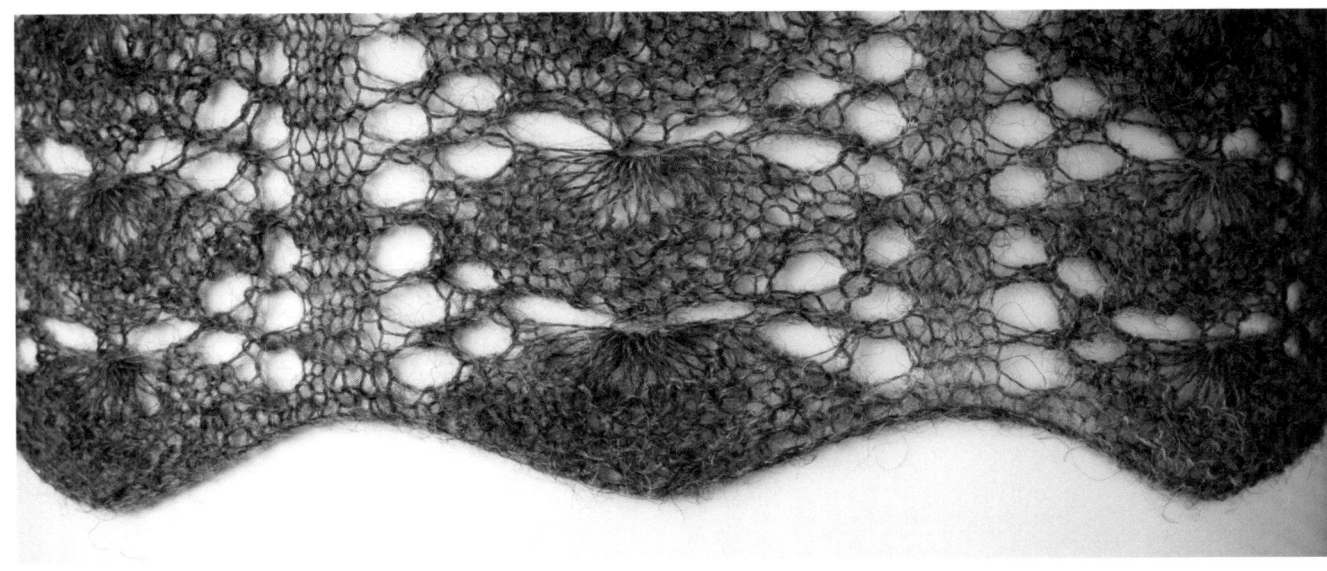

Sky and Sea Scarf

We are in seventeen-foot-long, twenty-three-inch-wide sea kayaks, steering as much with our hips as with our paddles. Angus Nicol, of Sea Kayak Shetland, does this all the time. But we don't. He makes sure that folk such as us who maybe have a little kayak experience on the flatwater of a man-made lake in Oklahoma are as safe and comfortable as possible when paddling the waters of the North Atlantic.

Angus is as much a nature and history guide as he is a kayak guide. The kayak seems to be a means to an end, rather than an end in itself. Of course, riding the waves and swells of the ocean is fun, but a kayak is also a way to get out of one's element and into someone else's. That someone else in the waters off of Shetland might be a seal or an otter or a puffin. The wildlife is abundant.

We have put the kayaks in the water off the Isle of West Burra. It is calm here today. Soon a small pod of seals takes interest. They poke their heads above water, and we keep still, allowing them to figure out our intentions. My intention is not to be beaten up by a seal, but I needn't be worried.

Angus guides us back and forth across the voe. On one side sits an abandoned stone building that he says would have been inhabited fifty years ago. Now only sheep seem to be interested.

As we paddle along, the calm waters become a little more active. At first we could have been on a lake at home, but now we're aware that we are on big, big water, and it's alive. The swells are perhaps four feet tall. We rise and fall with ease because the kayaks are made for this. On shore, though, waves crash into rock. We steer clear of the breaks. Angus points to the southwest. "Next land…Florida."

Angus has us follow him into a sea cave after checking it out first himself. It is dark and tight inside. The cave doesn't go through, so we find ourselves turning seventeen-foot kayaks around in a twenty-five-foot-wide cave.

Back out in the open water, I spot a fence built right up to and hanging off a cliff eighty feet above the shore. I mention that it might need attention, and that I wouldn't want to be the one to work on it. Angus assures me that it is in fine condition and was built that way, but sheep will still find a way around it. He sometimes finds sheep that have fallen and returns them to their owners.

We've rounded a piece of land that sat across from where we put our kayaks in the water, and I start to wonder if we'll have to paddle back. We pull up to a small beach, portage the three kayaks over a fence, and put them in the water again. Angus's car is within sight. The seals welcome us back.

A seal rests on a rock while watching a passing kayak, and Angus Nicol of Sea Kayak Shetland rests while watching for passing seals.

The themes of sky and sea are frequently represented in Shetland designs. Would you expect anything less from the beautiful but hard-to-reach islands located where the Atlantic Ocean meets the North Sea?

From colorful puffins to eider ducks, fowl have long been a draw for visitors to Shetland. The sea, filled with herring, seals, otters, and colorful non-vertebrate life forms, is part of everyday life there as well.

Kayaking with Angus Nicol and listening to his descriptions of the fowl and fish was one of my favorite activities when visiting Shetland. A naturalist as well as a kayaker, he educated us on his Shetland as we paddled around the peninsula known as East Burra.

No place on Shetland is farther than five miles from the sea. The two traditional Shetland stitches in this garment reflect the two constant themes of sky and sea.

Materials:

Yarns: Jamieson & Smith Shetland Supreme 1 ply Lace Weight Cobweb (2 balls)
Alternate Yarn: Lost City Knits North Pasture Alpaca Lace Weight (2 skeins)
Yardage: 600 yds 549 / meters (J&S); 550 yds / 503 meters (LCK)
Colors Shown in Samples: Grey and Black (J&S); Artemesia and Extra Virgin (LCK)
Needle Size: 3 US / 3.25 mm (J&S) ; 4 US / 3.25 mm (LCK) circular needle
Finished Size: approximately 17 inches / 43 cm x 56 inches / 142 cm

BASIC INSTRUCTIONS

Sky and Sea Scarf is knit using two traditional Shetland stitches, creating a garter stitch background. There is patterning on both the right side (RS) and the wrong side (WS) of the fabric.

Begin Bird's Eye Chart

Cast on 57 stitches using the provisional cast on of your choice. Personally, I like to use Judy's Magic Cast On as a provisional for this particular scarf. This method requires you to cast on the appropriate stitch count on both needles. If you do this, begin stitching into one needle, leaving the stitches on the other needle live, but suspended until you need them later. An extra needle or cable from an interchangeable needle is handy for this maneuver.

Some knitters prefer to slip the first stitch on every row (RS and WS). I highly recommend this trick, which makes it easier to pick up stitches later.

Knit 4 rows of garter stitch. The first and last 3 stitches per side will be your garter stitch edging. The edging stitches are not charted; separate them using stitch markers, and be sure to mark the RS of your fabric for easy reference. This pattern has increases and decreases on both sides of the fabric. Work the decreases in the direction the symbols lean whether you are on the RS or the WS.

Bird's Eye

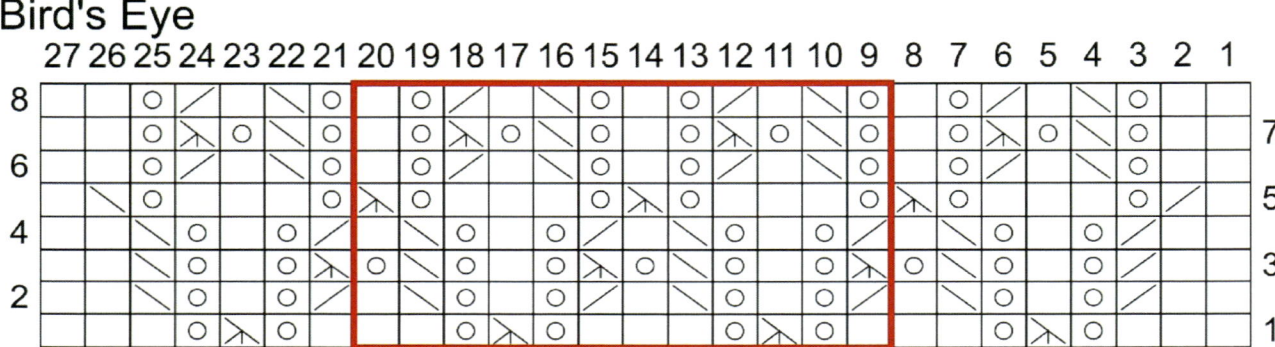

Work 46 repeats of the 8 rows of the Bird's Eye chart for a nice long scarf, then knit 4 rows of garter stitch. Do not bind off.

If you are changing colors for the edging, cut your yarn leaving a 6-inch tail, then change to the new color.

Pick up and knit 1 stitch for every 2 rows (or every slipped stitch) along one long side. Recover the live stitches from the provisional cast on, and knit into each of these stitches. Pick up and knit 1 stitch for every 2 rows (or every slipped stitch) along the second long side. Knit into every stitch of the last garter stitch row. (490 stitches total)

Work 1 round of *p2tog, yo*.
Knit 1 round even. Cut yarn, leaving a 6-inch tail.

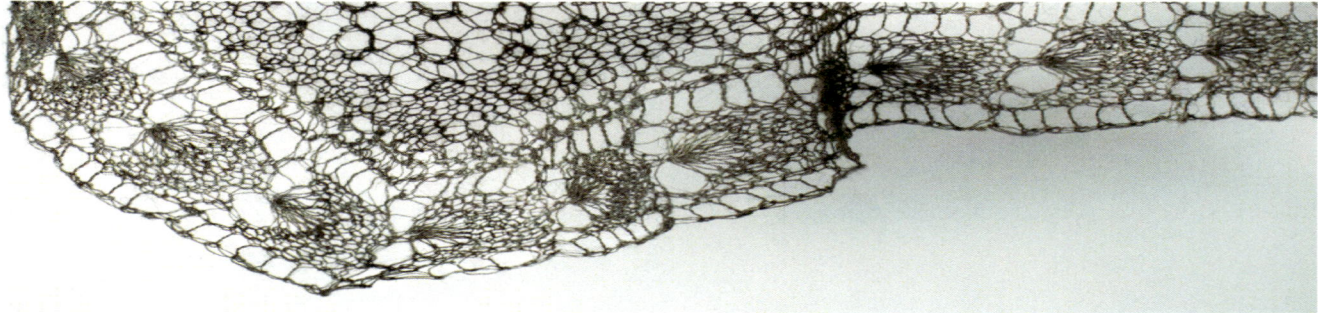

Begin the Cockleshell Edging Chart

Using a provisional method (the Invisible Cast On is a good choice for this situation), cast on 12 stitches. Row 1 begins at the outer edge of the border and returns to the body of the scarf while knitting in pattern. You will be knitting the first and purling the second stitch of the double yarn over on each subsequent row. This chart, like the body of the scarf, creates a garter stitch fabric.

Cockleshell Edging

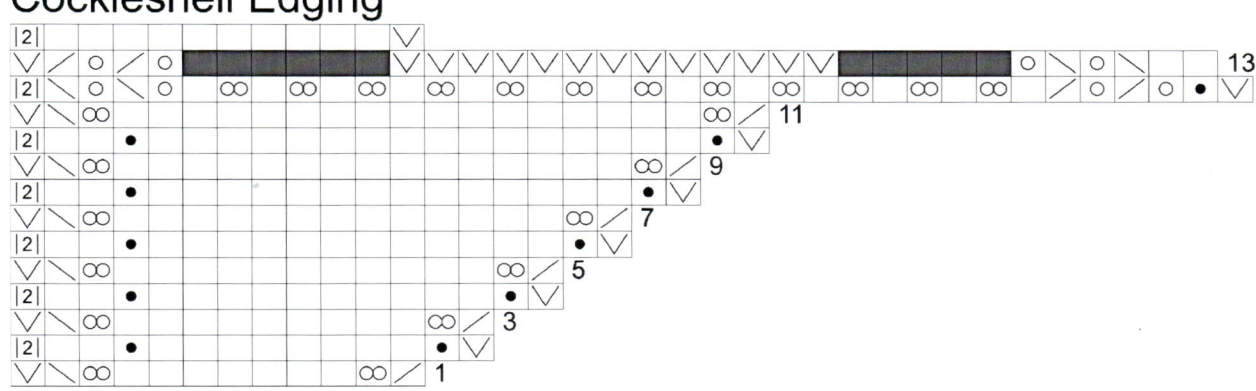

No stitch

k

● p

∨ s1

○ yo

∕ k2tog

∖ ssk

⋋ s1-k2tog-psso

∞ Double YO

|2| Join 2 together

IMPORTANT INSTRUCTION NOTE:

When slipping the purled stitches on Row 13, drop the double yarn overs between the 13 purled stitches, being sure to slip the purled stitch after the last double yarn over for a total of 13 slipped stitches. Transfer the 13 stitches back to the left needle, **THEN** purl the cluster together as one stitch before executing the rest of the stitches on that row. It is a tricky maneuver; take the time to make sure every one of the slipped stitches is caught when purling them together. A dropped stitch can ruin the exacting work you've accomplished.

Work 70 repeats of the 14 rows of the Cockleshell Edging Chart. When all 70 of the cockleshells that surround the scarf have been worked, remove the provisional cast on and recover the live stitches to a second needle. Graft the cast on and the last row of the edging together using the Kitchener stitch. Weave in ends after blocking.

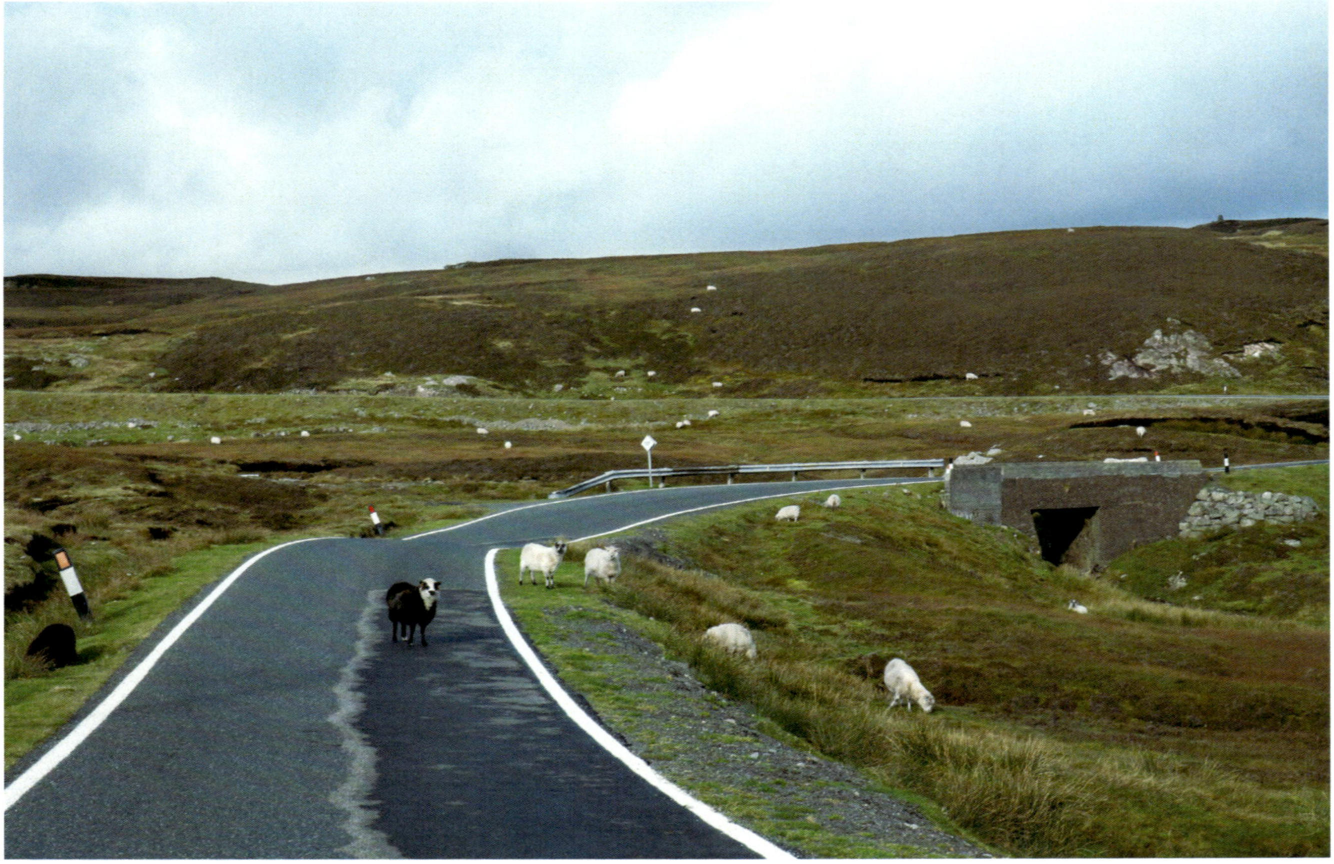

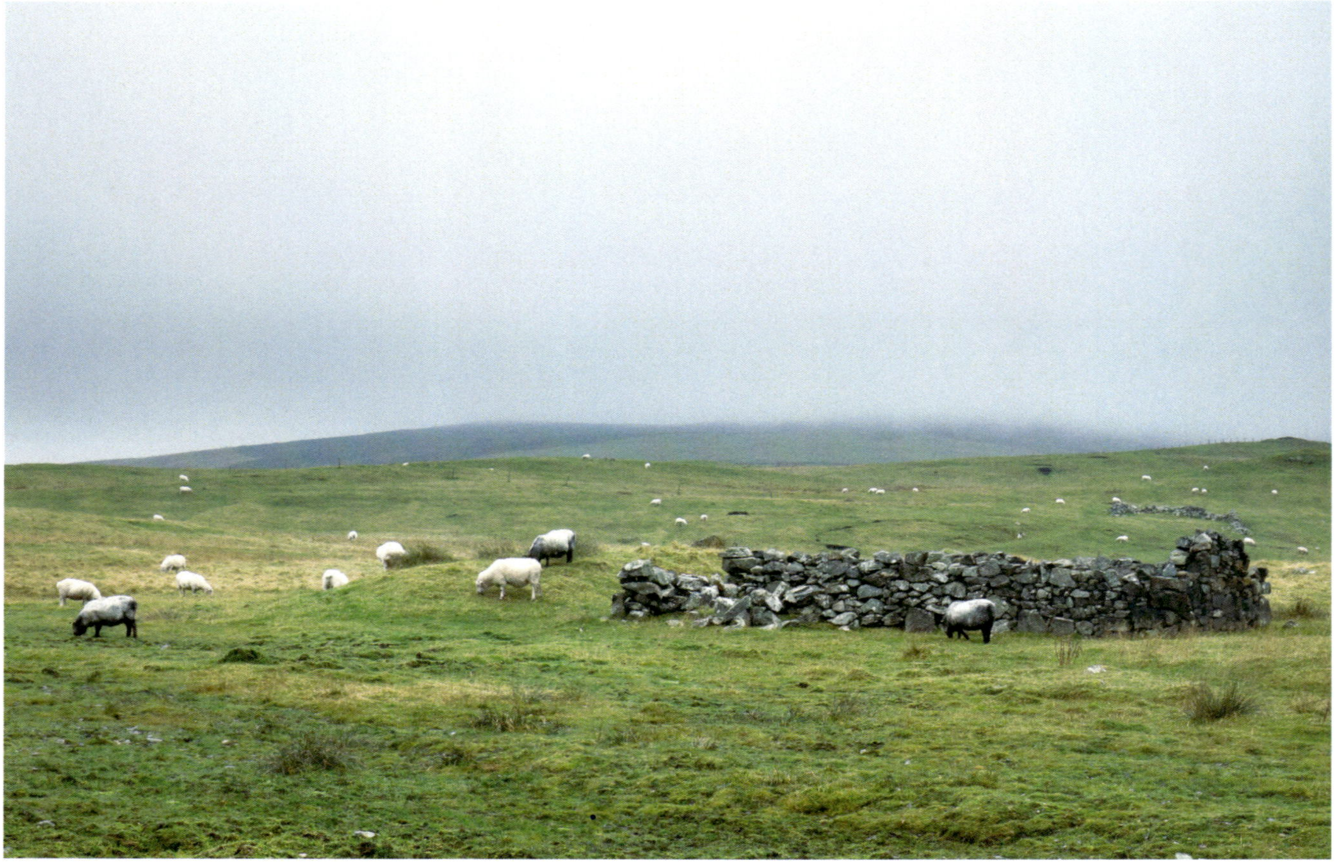

Kailyard Shawl

When the new road was being paved downhill from Barbara Fraser's croft south of Lerwick, the lifelong Shetlander knew not to let natural resources go to waste. As large machinery came through, tearing up bedrock for the new, smooth surface, she went down with a cart and carried the newly unearthed stones up her narrow driveway. In a matter of years, she turned the pile of stones into a rock wall surrounding her garden, or kailyard, as the Shetlanders say.

The walls are spectacular. One doesn't get the impression that Barbara is particularly proud of the walls, however, despite their being quite an achievement. Shetlanders are practical folk. Nothing is done for fancy, except perhaps for exquisite lace and colorful Fair Isle, but Barbara isn't a knitter. The walls are there to keep her sheep away from the kale.

If the walls are spectacular, the kale is even more so. During a mid-October visit, after a summer that never got warm enough for an ideal garden, the kale plants in Barbara's yard are huge. They're the talk of the island.

She is mostly modest about her achievement but offers a Shetland cookbook with a picture of her behind a wheelbarrow of prize-winning kale overflowing the width of the cart. The competition was supposed to be for overall crop production, but her kale was so impressive it took the prize.

Her secret is seaweed. When the wind and tides are right, she drives her four-wheel utility vehicle to the beach and gathers as much as she can carry. It can't be as hard to move as the stone was, although perhaps it's more slippery to handle. She starts thousands of young kale one year in small patches, sells some of these in the spring, and puts her plants out earlier than most.

She will mix the harvested kale with potatoes that she also grows, mix in some spices, and feed the concoction to her sheep. She doesn't bother with sheep dogs. They're too hard to train, certainly harder than cooking her kale and training the sheep to come to her for a bite to eat.

She will gather seeds from the best plants and hang bags of seed above the stove in her sitting room to dry over the winter. Soon, she'll start it all again.

(Above) Stone walls protect young kale seedlings from hungry sheep and Shetland winds. (Left) Barbara Fraser on the scooter she uses to get around Shetland, and when it was new, took on a tour of the Highlands of Scotland with a gallon of fuel strapped to the back.

Kailyard Shawl

Off and on throughout my life I have turned the earth to garden, sometimes planting vegetables, flowers, or herbs. The satisfaction from raising a small garden plot involves becoming one with the earth, water, and pollinators, and tending to plants as they transition from first blossoms to supplying an essential element of life – food.

In years that I haven't raised vegetables, shopping for fresh and locally grown produce led me to become a customer at the local farmer's market in Tulsa, Oklahoma. Farmers and backyard gardeners of all ages set up booths in the wee hours of Saturday mornings, putting out the produce and flowers they have harvested in the days and hours before the market. It's a diverse group, but they all believe that fresh food is best, and are willing to work hard to make it happen.

This shawl contains motifs of Shetland's rock walls, bees, blossoms, vines, and waves. I felt a circular shawl, in this case a pi shawl, to be a fitting tribute to gardening, one of the simplest earthly pleasures.

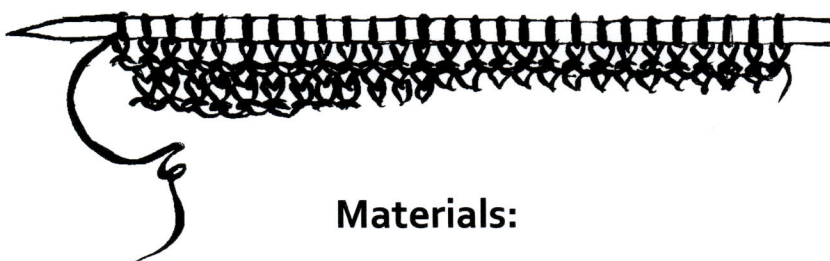

Materials:

Suggested Yarn: Lost City Knits North Pasture Alpaca (5 skeins)
Alternate Yarn: Jamieson & Smith Shetland Supreme 2 Ply Lace Weight (11 balls)
Yardage: 2300 yards / 2100 meters
Color Shown in Sample: Cerrillos, Promise of Spring, Cocksure, and Extra Virgin
Needle Size: 4 US / 3.5 mm double point needles for cast on and 4 US / 3.5 mm circular needles in a variety of lengths
Finished Size: 64 inches / 162 cm diameter

BASIC INSTRUCTIONS

Kailyard is a circular shawl, knit from the center out. The finished size of this shawl is quite large. A small circular shawl is difficult to wear, but a large one offers several options. Some people prefer to fold a circular shawl in half, and some simply fold under ¼ at the neck and use a shawl pin or brooch as a closure, allowing the full pattern to be visible as it drapes. If you haven't tried this method, I highly encourage you to give it a whirl – and I do mean whirl! That is one of the delights of a large pi shawl – whirling! Consider it your personal superhero cape.

All even-numbered rest rounds are uncharted knit stitches **EXCEPT** for the Lapping Waves chart, in which even-numbered rows are wrong-side (WS) rows, and therefore the typical symbols are reversed – for example the typical symbol for the knit stitch (empty cell) is worked as a purl stitch and the typical symbol for the purl stitch (dark dot) is worked as a knit stitch.

There are 6 charts for this pattern. Be sure to read notes in red text before casting on to avoid an error.

Begin at the Center

Cast on 8 stitches using whatever cast on you are comfortable with. I like the Emily Ocker method for a square or round shawl. Divide the 8 stitches onto 4 double-point needles (dpns). *This counts as Round 1.* Join to knit in the round: 2 stitches per dpn. This may be fiddly for a few rounds, but before you know it you'll have enough stitches to put the entire shawl on a single circular needle.

Round 2 - Increase – work *yo, k* around. (16 stitches)
Knit 3 rounds even.

Round 6 - Increase – work *yo, k* around. (32 stitches)
Knit 5 rounds even.

Round 12 - Increase – work *yo, k* around. (64 stitches)
Knit 2 rounds even.
Work Rounds 1-6 of **Stone Fence** chart 1 time - 16 times around.
Knit 3 rounds even.

Round 24 - Increase – work *yo, k* around. (128 stitches)
Knit 3 rounds even.
Work Rounds 1-6 of **Fish Tail** Chart 3 times - 16 times around.
Knit 2 rounds even.

Round 48 - Increase – work *yo, k* around. (256 stitches)
Knit 5 rounds even.
Work Rounds 1-12 of **Bumble Bees** Chart 3 times - 32 times around. Work Rounds 1-6 again.
(This chart contains a double yarn over. On the subsequent rest round, knit into the first yarn over, purl into the second. On Rounds 7,9, and 11 the double yarn over straddles the marker for the beginning of the round. Be sure to purl the first yarn over of the round and knit the last to remain consistent.)
Knit 1 round even.

Round 96 - Increase – work *yo, k* around (512 stitches)
Knit 4 rounds even.
Work Rounds 1-16 of **Blossoms** chart 5 times - 64 times around. Work chart Rounds 1-8 again. *(Red lines mark pattern repeat. This chart calls for slipping 1 stitch (1 time only) from the previous round at the beginning of Round 9, and returning that slipped stitch on Round 15.)*
Knit 3 rounds even.

Round 192 - Increase – work *yo, k* around (1024 stitches)
Knit 1 round even.
Work Rounds 1-12 of **Vines and Leaves** chart 3 times, 64 times around. Work Rounds 1-10 again.
Knit 1 round even.
Knit 1 round, decreasing 2 stitches evenly. (1022 stitches)
Knit 2 rounds even. Cut yarn, leaving an 18-inch tail.

Stone Fence

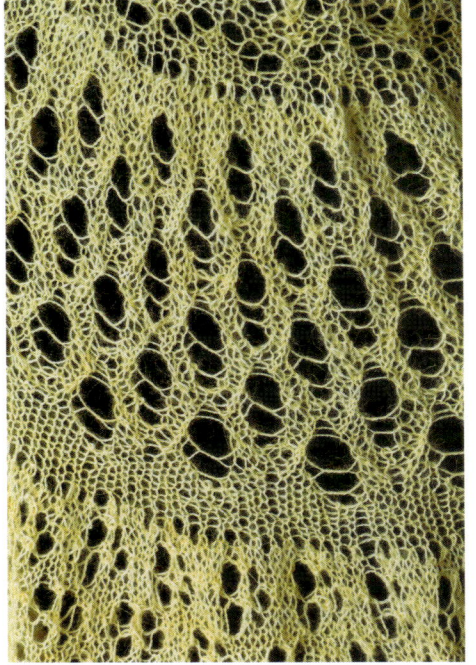

Fish Tail

Bumble Bees

Blossoms

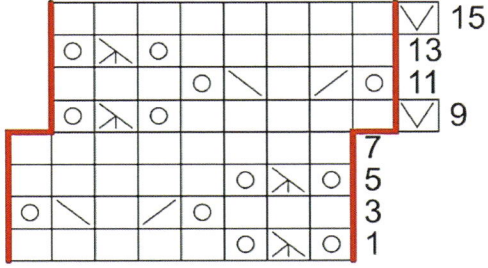

Vines and Leaves

Begin Lapping Waves Chart

Using the provisional cast on of your choice, cast on 13 stitches.

The next step can be tricky. Begin by knitting Row 1 (RS). For Row 2 (WS), begin by knitting the next stitch of the body of the shawl together with the first stitch of the edging. Every RS row of the Lapping Waves chart will end with a slipped stitch AND the first stitch of every WS row will be purled together with the next stitch on the body of the shawl. Continue working the Lapping Waves chart around the entire shawl. You will work a total of 146 Lapping Waves.

End with RS Row 13. Cut yarn, leaving an 18-inch tail. Remove the provisional cast on, and return the 13 live stitches to a second needle. Graft the cast on and the last row of the edging together using the Kitchener stitch. Weave in ends after blocking.

Lapping Waves

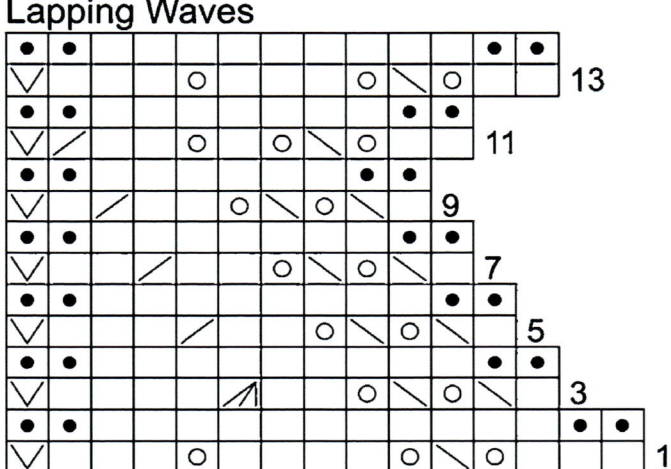

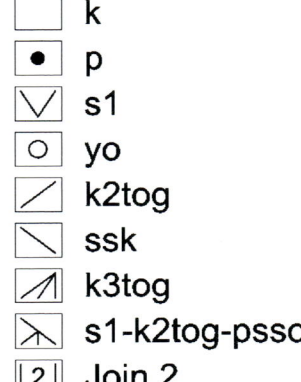

Stitches

k	
•	p
V	s1
o	yo
/	k2tog
\	ssk
⟋|	k3tog
⋊	s1-k2tog-psso
|2|	Join 2

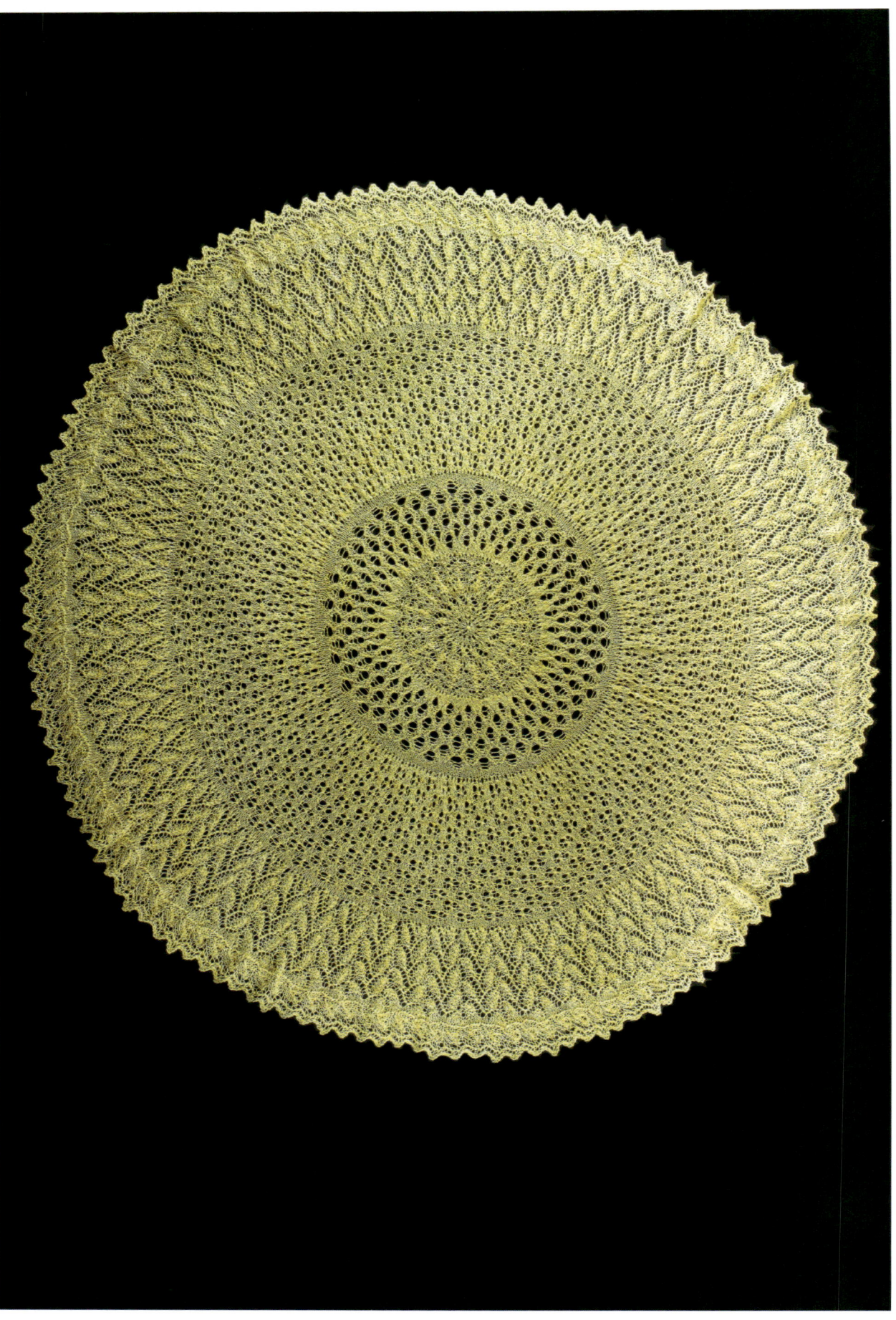

A Brief Note About Patterns

The preceding pages consist of five lace patterns, several with alternative charts which create a different version of the garment. These patterns were inspired by the people and environment of Shetland. Each contains a brief design synopsis. All of the patterns are charted, with some written text and helpful hints. A legend of stitches used is included for each pattern, and often for each individual chart.

I've included patterns in a variety of shapes. Who wants to knit the same shape over and over? Each pattern includes several suggested yarns, both from Lost City Knits and from Jamieson & Smith Shetland Wool Brokers, in weights ranging from cobweb to (jumper) fingering weight.

Because these patterns are lace an exact gauge is not crucial, but your final measurements and yardage may vary if you are an overly tight or loose knitter. Needle sizes are suggestions, and are provided because they gave the desired hand of fabric to the sample shawls.

Below is a key of the stitch abbreviations used throughout the book. Please read through each pattern fully before casting on.

RS	Right side of fabric	WS	Wrong side of fabric
k	Knit	yo	Wrap the working yarn around the right needle, from front to back (counter clockwise) (single increase).
p	Purl	double yo	Wrap the working yarn around the right needle twice, from front to back (counter clockwise) (double increase).
s1	Slip 1 stitch from the left to the right needle without knitting or twisting the stitch.	k2tog	Knit 2 stitches together (single right leaning decrease).
ssk	Slip 2 stitches separately knitwise, move stitches back to the left needle, then knit the slipped stitches together.	k2tog-b	Knit 2 stitches together through the back of the loop (single left-leaning decrease).
kfb	Knit in the front and back of a stitch.	k3tog	Knit 3 stitches together (double right-leaning decrease).
No Stitch	This stitch does not exist on your needle. Ignore the cell in the chart and move to the next stitch.	Join 2	Join 1 stitch from the body of the shawl with an edging stitch by purling them together.
s1k2togpsso	Slip 1 stitch knitwise, knit 2 stitches together, then pass the slipped stitch over the k2tog.	2/2 RC	Slip 2 stitches purlwise to cable needle and hold in back; k2; k2 from cable needle.
1/2 LC	Slip 1 stitch purlwise to cable needle and hold in front; k2; k1 from cable needle.	1/2 RC	Slip 2 stitches purlwise to cable needle and hold in back; k1; k2 from cable needle.
3/2 RC	Slip 2 stitches purlwise to cable needle and hold in back; k3; k2 from cable needle.	3/2 LC	Slip 3 stitches purlwise to cable needle and hold in front; k2; k3 from cable needle.

Schematic Sketches

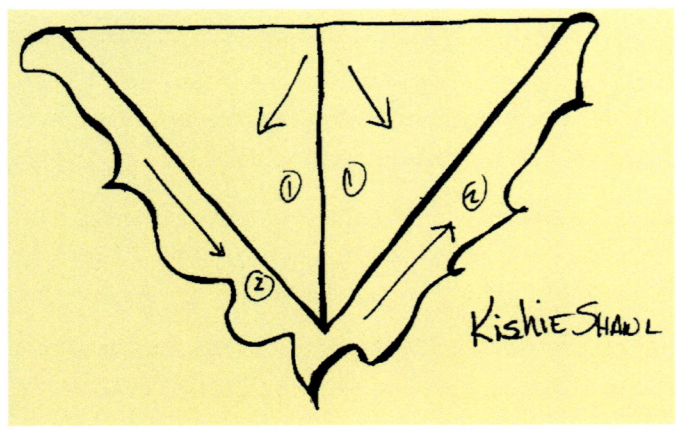

A top-down triangle shawl with an applied edging.

A center-square shawl, picked up along all four sides then knit in the round, with an applied edging

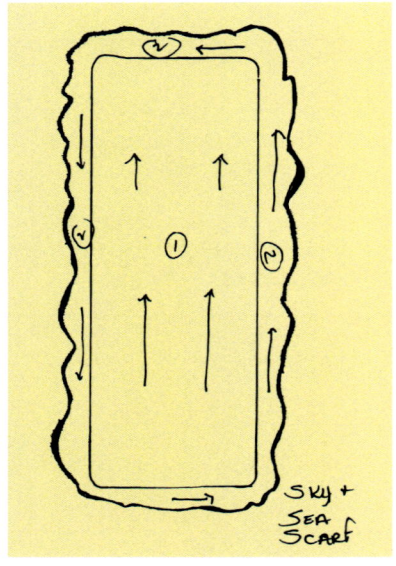

A rectangle scarf knit from end to end, with an applied edging along all four sides.

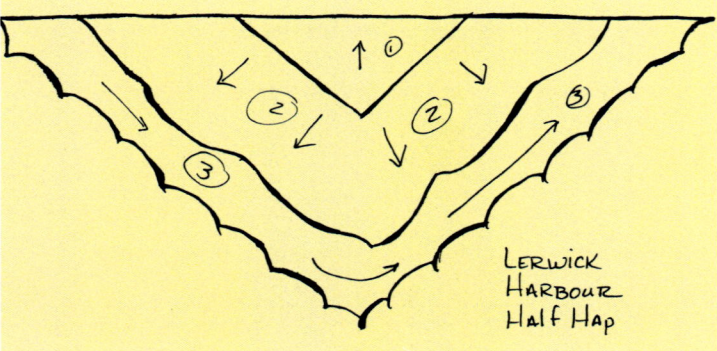

A triangle shawl from the center point to the top, picked up and knit flat across the lower sides, with an applied edging.

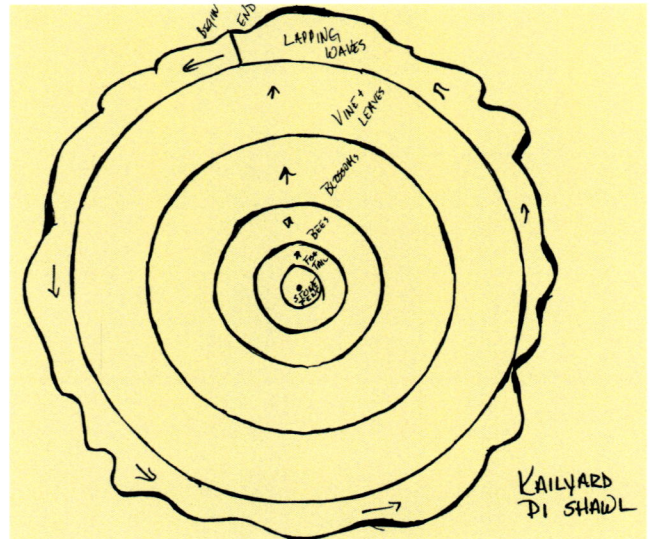

A pi shawl knit from the center out, with an applied edging.

Acknowledgements

We would like to thank Karen and Barbara Fraser, Mary and Tommy Isbister, Angus and Wendy Nicol, Elizabeth Johnston, Ella Gordon, Amy Gair, Oliver Henry, Roisin McAtamney, and Donna Smith in Shetland. The Lost City Knits test-knit team for Ultima Thule consisted of Laurie Remenyi, Jessica Jones, and Maria Hart, and we couldn't have gotten the patterns right without their patience and assistance. Closer to home we would like to thank Mike Kimrey and Sarah Peasley for help with editing, Hillarey Dees for help with layout, Danny Cook for teaching Denise the knit stitch, Stephanie Asbury Baker for many of the stitches that followed, and Chris's father, Paul Dykes, who would have liked this a lot.

Chris took all of the photos with the exception of pages 37, 38, and 42, which are from Sea Kayak Shetland, and the back cover, which is from Alamy. The Shetland Museum provided the photos on pages 8, 16, 28, 36, and 44.

All sketches, schematics, and hand lettering were done by Denise.

The following websites might be of interest:

www.shetland-museum.org.uk

www.seakayakshetland.co.uk

www.shetlandhandspun.com

www.ellagordon.wordpress.com

www.amygair.wordpress.com

www.shetlanddialect.org.uk

Denise discovered that she was a natural-born knitter in her forties. After a trip to the Taos Wool Festival she returned and told Chris that she wanted to dye yarn. "Sure. What's the worst that could happen?" Chris asked her. The couple now own and operate Lost City Knits from their farm in northeastern Oklahoma.

Shetlanders gather on a Friday night at the Mareel arts center in Lerwick. The venue offers two movie screens, a live theater auditorium, production rooms, and a café and bar. It's modern and high tech, but acknowledges Shetland's heritage by projecting a series of traditional stitches on the walls.